WHAT'S THE DEAL?

Crack and Cocaine

Karla Fitzhugh

Heinemann Library

Chicago, Illinois

Customer Service 888-454-2279
Visit our website at www.heinemannlibrary.com

For more information address the publisher:
Heinemann Library, 100 N. LaSalle, Suite 1200,
Chicago, IL 60602

Produced for Heinemann Library by
White-Thomson Publishing Ltd,
Bridgewater Business Centre,
210 High Street, Lewes,
East Sussex BN7 2NH,
United Kingdom.

Consultant: Jenny McWhirter, Head of Education and
    Prevention, DrugScope
Editorial: Clare Collinson
Design: Tim Mayer
Picture Research: Amy Sparks
Production: Duncan Gilbert

Originated by P.T. Repro Multi Warna
Printed and bound in China, by South China
    Printing Company.

10 09 08 07 06
10 9 8 7 6 5 4 3 2 1

**Library of Congress Cataloging-in-
Publication Data**
Fitzhugh, Karla.
  Crack and cocaine / Karla Fitzhugh.
    p. cm. -- (What's the deal?)
  Includes bibliographical references and index.
  ISBN 1-4034-7028-6 (hc)
  1. Crack (Drug)--Juvenile literature.
  2. Cocaine--Juvenile literature.
  I. Title. II. Series.
  RC568.C6F58 2005
  362.29'8--dc22
                          2005001612

Acknowledgments
The publishers would like to thank the following for
permission to reproduce photographs:

Alamy 7 (David Hoffman Photo Library), 16 (John
Rensten), 22 (Janine Wiedel Photolibrary), 32
(Photofusion Picture Library), 38 (Jack Sullivan),
41 (Paul Doyle), 42 (Jeff Greenberg); Corbis 8–9
(Gustavo Gilabert/Corbis Saba), 10 (Greg Smith), 11
(Jacques M. Chenet), 14 (Reuters), 17 (John Henley),
19 (Lawrence Manning), 24–25 (Lester Lefkowitz), 34
(Brooks Kraft), 36 (Rob Howard), 44 (Reuters); Getty
Images 4–5 (Stone), 13 (The Image Bank), 21 (The
Image Bank), 37 (Taxi), 39 (AFP), 46 (Stone), 47 (Taxi),
48–49 (Stone), 50–51 (Stone); Harcourt 30–31;
photolibrary.com 23 (plainpicture), 28–29 (Gary
Sheppard), 35 (Gategno), 40 (Claber Carroll); Rex
Features 6 (Andy Drysdale), 12 (Globe Photos Inc.),
26 (Kip Rano), 27 (YPP); Science Photo Library 20
(Oscar Burrell); Topfoto 45.

Cover artwork by Phil Weyman, Kralinator Design.

Every effort has been made to contact copyright
holders of any material reproduced in this book. Any
omissions will be rectified in subsequent printings if
notice is given to the publishers.

The case studies and quotations in this book are
based on factual examples. However, in some cases
the names or other personal information have been
changed to protect the privacy of the individual
concerned.

The paper used to print this book comes from
sustainable resources.

Contents

▌ Some words are shown in bold, **like this.** You can find out what they mean by looking in the glossary.

Danni was fifteen and at a party, having a good time with his friends. He knew there were some people there using drugs, but he didn't want to use them.

"It made me feel quite uncomfortable. Someone came up and asked us if we wanted to buy some drugs—ecstasy, cocaine, or anything. He was just a regular looking guy—not a sinister drug **dealer** type. I felt pretty nervous. I know drugs are illegal and I don't want to mess up my future. Also, I know I really don't

need drugs to have a great time. So I told him that I did not want to buy anything. He tried to push me—but I said no again, very firmly. He went away and didn't ask me again. I know it might happen to me like that another time. But I'll know how to deal with it."

What would you have done if you were Danny? How would you have handled the situation?

Cocaine and crack are illegal drugs that have strong effects on the body and mind. **Abusing** these drugs is very dangerous. Many people end up in the hospital after using crack and cocaine, and every year people die after using them. Some users find it very hard to quit using these drugs. This can seriously affect their studies and wreck important relationships. Being caught with crack or cocaine can also lead to trouble with the police or even time in prison. This can ruin a promising career and prevent someone from traveling abroad.

Making decisions

You might think that crack and cocaine will never be an issue for you, but one day you may be offered these drugs by someone you know or by a dealer. Do you know what you would say? This book gives you the information you need to help you make your own decisions about crack and cocaine. It looks at the illegal trade in these drugs and considers the short-term and long-term risks of using them. There are also many issues to think about. What part do the **media** play in making these drugs seem evil or glamorous? What is the right way to deal with drug abuse and what help is available for **addicts**? Get ready to find out—what's the deal with crack and cocaine?

▮ Cocaine powder is often chopped with a razor blade or credit card and arranged into thin lines before being used.

Cocaine and crack are powerful **stimulants** that speed up some of the actions of the brain. Cocaine may appear as a powder, or in a purified form known as crack.

What are stimulants?

Stimulants are drugs that speed up a person's brain activity, making them feel more awake or alert. They work by increasing the amounts of certain chemicals in the brain, which affects a person's feelings and thoughts and other processes in the rest of the body. There are many different types of stimulants. Some, such as caffeine (found in coffee, tea, and some soft drinks), have mild effects. Others, such as crack and cocaine, have much stronger effects.

▌People often use a rolled-up dollar bill or a straw to help them sniff lines of cocaine.

▌ Crack is usually sold in the form of small raisin-sized lumps, known as rocks.

Cocaine powder

The most common form of cocaine is a white powder made up of tiny crystals. The chemical name for this powder is **cocaine hydrochloride**. It is typically sold in small paper bags, or "wraps," containing about 0.35 ounces (one gram) of cocaine. Most users divide cocaine into thin lines on a flat surface, using a razor blade or credit card. They then **snort** the drug up the nose. The drug is quickly absorbed through the soft tissues inside the nose and carried in the bloodstream to the brain. Some users rub any cocaine that is left over on to their gums, so it will be absorbed into the bloodstream. Sometimes, users dissolve cocaine powder in water and inject the drug.

What is crack?

Crack, or **freebase** cocaine, is a form of cocaine hydrochloride that has been processed so it can be smoked. It is normally smoked in a pipe, a glass tube, a plastic bottle, or foil. It gets its name from the cracking noises that are made as it is smoked. Crack is a more concentrated form of cocaine than cocaine powder. Because it is smoked, the drug enters the bloodstream and reaches the brain more quickly than when cocaine powder is snorted. This means that the effects of crack are felt more quickly and strongly than the effects of cocaine powder. Like cocaine powder, crack is sometimes turned into a liquid and injected.

⚠ Street terms for cocaine and crack

Street names for cocaine include: blow, coke, Charlie, C, dust, gak, snow, toot, white, Colombian marching powder, jazz salt, and nose candy.

Street names for crack include: rock, stones, gravel, base, freebase, and wash.

Cocaine is made from the leaves of the coca plant, which grows mainly in the Andes Mountains region of South America. It is mostly grown by poor farmers because it is the only crop that makes them enough money to live. The leaves of the coca plant are processed to make the powder form of cocaine.

Where the cocaine story begins

Coca grows mainly in the South American countries of Colombia, Bolivia, and Peru. People who live in this mountainous region have grown the plant for centuries and have used it traditionally as a medicine and in religious ceremonies. People chew the leaves, which have a mild stimulant effect, to help them cope with hunger, tiredness, and pain. It is also used to make a tea called *maté de coca*.

Why do people grow coca?

It is legal to grow a certain amount of coca for traditional uses in South America, but most coca grown in the region today is produced illegally to be made into cocaine. Many small farms in South America grow coca illegally because they cannot make enough money from growing legal crops, such as coffee. Without the money they get from growing coca, they may be unable to buy enough food or provide proper housing, clothing, or education for their children. The farmers who grow coca still make very little money. Refining coca into cocaine to sell is the most profitable part of the cocaine trade.

Production of cocaine

When the coca leaves have been picked, they are put into a tank, mixed with certain chemicals, and mashed up. This makes a paste called *basuco*. This paste is sometimes smoked by people in South America, and it has stronger effects than simply chewing the leaves. The chemicals that end up in the paste can severely damage the smokers' lungs. Most of the *basuco* is sent to illegal processing plants or factories, where it is treated to make a purer form of the drug, called cocaine hydrochloride. This is the form of cocaine that is then transported to other countries. Crack is usually made in the country it is sold in, often in small secret "laboratories" or kitchens.

▌Coca plants are one of the few crops that grow well in the soil of the Andes Mountains.

⚠ Producing crack

Cocaine hydrochloride is a type of salt, formed by a chemical reaction between the cocaine and an acid. Crack is made by removing the acid and "freeing" the alkaloid base from the salt. This is why crack is sometimes known as freebase cocaine.

9

The worldwide trade in cocaine has made the criminal gangs who control it very rich and powerful, and the business has brought violence and murder to many communities. The drugs are illegally transported around the world via a number of different routes.

Drug cartels

Poor farmers only make a small amount of money from growing and selling coca leaves. However, the cocaine trade is a multimillion-dollar business. The trade in cocaine is organized mainly by criminal gangs, or **cartels**, in South America. The **drug barons** who control these gangs have made enormous fortunes, profiting from the distribution and sale of cocaine around the world.

Some cartels employ small armies of soldiers to protect themselves or to force people to carry out their illegal orders. There are reports of murders, torture, and people vanishing without a trace when they try to stand up against these gangs. Some cartels are so powerful that the governments in their own countries can do little to stop them.

International distribution

Moving cocaine illegally between countries is known as smuggling or **trafficking**. Smugglers use several different methods to move drugs around, either in large or small amounts. One of the main routes for cocaine trafficking is from Colombia to the United States. Most of

■ A border patrol agent uses a specially trained dog to search for drugs in cars and trucks crossing into the United States from Mexico.

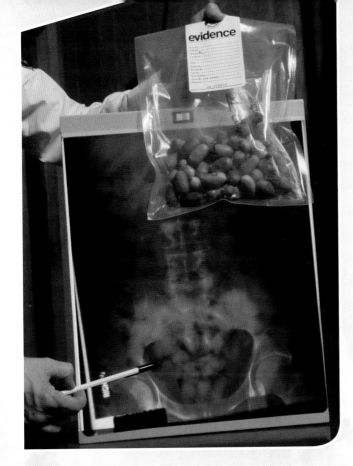

I This X ray, exhibited by a U.S. customs officer, shows a smuggler's stomach filled with small packets of drugs, which are displayed in the clear plastic bag.

the cocaine in the United States is smuggled in across the land border between Mexico and the United States. Some cocaine is also taken directly to the United States by small plane or by boat. The other main route for trafficking cocaine is from South America to Europe, via the Caribbean or African countries such as Nigeria. Most cocaine that enters Europe is smuggled into Spain and the Netherlands.

Drug mules

Criminal gangs find many ways to smuggle cocaine into other countries. Sometimes they use **couriers** or "**mules**." These people hide drugs in their luggage or clothing or inside their bodies. Sometimes they swallow many small packages of cocaine, wrapped in plastic or latex, so that the drugs are hidden inside their stomachs. This is very dangerous and can have serious consequences. If one of these packages breaks inside a person's body, the person could die from a cocaine **overdose**. Most of these people are very poor, and some say they are forced into smuggling drugs, either because they owe money to the gangs or because family members have been threatened with violence.

When people first come into contact with cocaine or crack, it is often through someone they know. However, behind the scenes, there is a whole network of dealers controlled by the criminal gangs that run the cocaine business.

The chain of dealers

Once supplies of cocaine have been smuggled into a country, they are sold to dealers. Dealing operates on many levels, but all drug dealers sell cocaine and crack to make money. The dealers at the top of the chain make huge profits, while the dealers at the bottom of the chain,

❙ Crack tends to be sold in small amounts. Before selling the drug, dealers often divide crack rocks into tiny glass containers known as vials.

■ Some cocaine and crack users buy from large-scale dealers who may be part of a criminal gang. However, most people come into contact with cocaine through people they already know.

who are selling drugs on the street, get much smaller profits.
Some of these dealers are drug users themselves, and deal drugs because they are desperate for money or because they need a regular supply of a drug.

Dealers often sell a range of drugs, and they work hard to sell drugs such as crack and cocaine to young people. They know that once someone has tried these drugs there is a good chance that they will become addicted. This will provide the dealer with a regular source of income.

Cocaine and crack from friends

Many people first start using cocaine or crack when they are offered the drugs by their friends or by other people they know. They may be at a friend's house, at a party, or at another social event where drugs are being passed around. Just because someone is given drugs by a friend, it does not mean that the drugs are safe to take. Also, even if no money is involved, it is still against the law to pass drugs on to other people.

"If I am offered cocaine I don't say 'No, I don't do that.' I say 'No, I can't party tonight because I have things to do tomorrow morning.' It's a lie, but it shuts them up."

Bethany, age seventeen. Most people say no if they are offered illegal drugs. If a dealer sees that someone is not interested, he or she will usually stop bothering the person.

The way cocaine and crack are dealt with in newspapers and magazines and on television shows can be confusing. One minute the message seems to be that these drugs are evil and dangerous; the next minute the drugs are made to seem popular and glamorous.

The full story?

Newspaper and magazine articles often talk about cocaine use among celebrities, but the reports only show a small part of the whole picture. Some reports seem to glamorize cocaine by suggesting it is part of the lifestyle of the rich and famous.

❚ American actor Robert Downey Jr. became a movie star in the 1980s, and he has made appearances in many successful TV shows. His battle with drug **dependence** and his arrests for cocaine-related offenses have been widely reported in the media.

Others use a "shock" approach to show how cocaine has damaged the lives of celebrities. In both cases, the subject of celebrity cocaine use is being used to sell newspapers or magazines. Reports in these publications rarely give accurate information about the effects of using the drug.

Scare stories

In the late 1980s and early 1990s, many news reports warned about the dangers of crack. They claimed that all users would be "hooked after the first **hit**." This information was not completely accurate, but some of the true health messages about the drug's dangers were not reported.

Some newspapers also published exaggerated reports claiming that babies born to pregnant crack users would be "genetically damaged" or "permanently handicapped." The truth is that babies born to people who use crack and cocaine are at risk of health problems, but there is no evidence that they are likely to suffer genetic damage or permanent disability.

Viewpoints

How should the **media** cover cocaine use? Some people think that the media's approach is irresponsible. Others say that the media should be free to report on drug use in any way they like.

- **The media should cover cocaine use in a more responsible way**

Reports in the media about celebrities using cocaine glamorize the drug and tempt people to use it. Some reports leave out important facts or contain inaccurate information. The media should stress that cocaine use is illegal and unhealthy and educate people about the risks.

- **It is not the media's job to influence the way people think about drugs**

The media's job is to report the news, not to educate the public about drugs. The media should be free to report the news in whatever way they like, to sell newspapers or attract viewers to a television program. It's up to schools and health organizations to educate people about drugs. Individuals should also educate themselves before making big decisions.

What do you think?

15

What sort of people use cocaine and crack? Cocaine is often associated with the rich and famous and crack with poorer people living in inner-city areas. But there is no "typical" cocaine or crack user, and in general most people have never used crack or cocaine.

▌Cocaine is often associated with celebrities and wealthy people, but cocaine use is no longer restricted to the rich.

Who uses cocaine?

Cocaine is often thought to be most popular among celebrities and other wealthy people. In recent years, however, the price of cocaine in some areas has fallen, and the drug is now used by people with a variety of backgrounds. In particular, the drug has become associated with the nightclub and all-night-party scene. It is sometimes used alongside, or instead of, ecstasy and other drugs. Students in universities and colleges also sometimes take cocaine at parties and **raves**.

Who smokes crack?

According to the 2003 National Survey on Drug Use and Health, about 7.9 million Americans ages 12 and older reported trying crack at least once during their lifetimes. This statistic represents about three percent of the population ages 12 and older. About 1.4 million people in this age group reported that they had used crack cocaine in the past year. About 604,000 reported using crack in the past month. According to

▌Cocaine and crack abuse can seriously affect a person's education and work prospects. This is one reason why so many people avoid using these drugs.

another survey from 2002 of several large cities in the United States, crack users tended to be young adults between the ages of 18 and 30.

Crack and cocaine statistics

A national survey taken in 2002 reported that an estimated 1.5 million Americans could be classified as being dependent on or abusing cocaine. Cocaine use steadily increased during the 1990s, reaching 1.2 million users in 2001. However, other surveys showed that crack and cocaine use among young people has decreased steadily in the early 2000s.

❗ What are the statistics?

- About 13 million people use cocaine—0.3 percent of the world's population between the ages of 15 and 65.

- In a 2003 survey, about 15 percent of young adults between 19 and 28 reported using cocaine at least once in their lifetime and 4.7 percent had used crack.

- A 2004 study conducted by the University of Michigan found that 8.1 percent of twelfth graders had tried cocaine at least once in their lifetimes.

Why Do People Use Cocaine and Crack?

In spite of the serious health risks, a few people are tempted to use crack and cocaine. So what influences the people who decide to use the drugs?

Reasons or excuses?

Sometimes, people may be tempted to try cocaine or crack out of curiosity or because they want to try something they think will be exciting. Others use crack or cocaine as part of a larger pattern of drug abuse, which may include using other illegal drugs or alcohol. They may use cocaine because they want to "wake up" after using other drugs that make them sleepy. Often these people do not know that mixing drugs in this way can kill.

Some people may be tempted to try crack or cocaine because they wrongly think it will help them escape from their problems. However, once the effects have worn off, the problems will still be there. Using crack or cocaine will only make a person's problems even harder to cope with.

Robert's story

Robert, an eighteen-year-old student, tried crack after being talked into it by someone at a party. Things didn't turn out as he'd been led to believe, and he doesn't plan to use it again.

"They said it would be the best feeling I'd ever experienced, and that it's not addictive. I believed them and I tried it. It wasn't what they made it out to be — the best feelings I've ever had are nothing to do with drugs. Within ten minutes I had strong **cravings**, *so I'm sure it's addictive."*

▌ Some people may feel pressured to try cocaine or crack if the drugs are being passed around among friends. It is not always easy for people to stick up for themselves and be different, but everyone should be free to make their own decisions about drugs.

Fitting in?

It is normal for people to want to fit in with friends, and sometimes they may copy their behavior so they feel like they are part of the group. They may be at a party where some people are using cocaine. They may think that if they do not join in they will feel left out. These situations can be hard to cope with. You will learn some suggestions on ways to deal with them later in the book.

Dealer pressure

Some people start to use crack or cocaine because they have been persuaded to try them by a dealer. Dealers can be very friendly and will say just about anything to get people to buy their drugs. Dealers know that once someone has tried crack or cocaine, there is a good chance that they will come back for more. However, if a dealer sees that someone is not interested, he or she will usually stop bothering them.

The Effects of Cocaine and Crack

Using crack or cocaine speeds up some of the reactions inside the brain, which causes changes in the body and in the way a user feels and behaves. When the effects wear off, users tend to experience many unpleasant feelings.

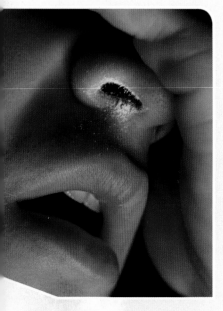

When a user snorts cocaine, the drug is absorbed through the soft tissues of the nose into the bloodstream. This can make the sensitive lining of the nose irritated and inflamed.

Question

How quickly are the effects of cocaine and crack felt?

Effects on the body

The effects of cocaine and crack on the body vary from person to person, but in most people:

- the body temperature, heart rate, and **blood pressure** increase
- the pupils dilate or widen
- the face becomes flushed or red
- if cocaine is snorted, the nose becomes runny, so the person sniffs a lot.

Cocaine also acts as a local **anesthetic**, making whatever it comes in contact with feel numb, such as the inside of the nose. Users may also get feelings of **nausea**, dizziness, and muscle twitches. Some users get an unpleasant feeling that insects are crawling under the skin. This is sometimes called "coke bugs."

Effects on feelings and behavior

Many users say that taking cocaine or crack gives them a **high** or a feeling of excitement. They may feel as if they are more awake and that they have more energy. They may also be more talkative than usual and feel more confident. The sensations are not always pleasant,

Once the effects of cocaine and crack wear off, the user experiences a range of unpleasant after-effects, such as tiredness and irritability. It's common for users to want to take more of the drug to avoid these feelings.

and can include feelings of anxiety and restlessness. Sometimes, users say things that seem overconfident or arrogant. If people have taken very large doses of cocaine or crack, they may behave strangely or aggressively.

After the drugs wear off

The high from snorting cocaine starts to wear off after about 15 to 30 minutes. The effects of crack wear off much more quickly— often within five or ten minutes. Initially, cocaine and crack cause the rapid release of dopamine, a chemical in the brain that causes pleasant sensations. By the time the effects have worn off, the amount of dopamine in some parts of the brain drops to a very low level and it takes the body a long time to build up the levels again. This leaves the user feeling exhausted, tense, and miserable.

Answer

Once it has been snorted, cocaine usually takes effect within a few minutes. When users inject cocaine or crack, or smoke crack, the effects are felt almost immediately.

Are Cocaine and Crack Addictive?

Cocaine and crack are powerfully addictive drugs. Many people become dependent on the way these drugs make them feel, so it can be very hard for users to stop taking them.

Becoming dependent

When people use cocaine or crack regularly, they gradually build up a **tolerance** to the effects of the drug. This means they need to take larger and more frequent doses to achieve the same effects. People can also become **psychologically dependent** on the effects of these drugs. They may use the drugs to get through everyday life and feel that they cannot cope without them. When people become dependent on cocaine or crack, they may gradually start to lose control of the amount they take and how often they take it. They may also spend a great deal of time thinking about drugs or trying to obtain more of them.

Question

Do all regular users become dependent?

Cravings and withdrawal

When users stop using cocaine or crack, they quickly start to feel tired and miserable and often experience strong **cravings** for more of the drug. These feelings become worse if people take the drugs in large doses and on a regular basis.

▌Users of crack experience very strong cravings when the effects of the drug wear off. This can mean that people who use crack may become dependent more quickly than people who use powder cocaine.

■ Some people who are dependent on cocaine or crack become so desperate for money to buy drugs that they resort to crime.

Users of crack rapidly develop particularly intense cravings, and often feel desperate for another **hit** after the drug's effects wear off.

When someone stops using cocaine or crack, they may experience **lethargy**, mood swings, and broken sleep patterns. In some cases they may suffer from severe depression. Some users experience symptoms such as vomiting, sweating, and diarrhea. Many people use more of the drug to avoid these unpleasant feelings, so it can be very hard for people to stop using cocaine or crack.

Effects of dependence

Dependence changes people's lives in many ways. Some people spend huge amounts of money on cocaine or crack. This can lead to serious money problems and some people turn to crime to fund their habit. They may steal money from family and friends or commit burglaries. Some users become involved in prostitution, earning money in return for sex.

Answer

Research suggests that between 10 and 15 percent of people who regularly use cocaine will become dependent within two to four years. A similar percentage of crack users are likely to become dependent, but it tends to happen within a few weeks or months, rather than years.

The Risks of Cocaine and Crack Abuse

Abuse of cocaine or crack has many serious health risks. Every year people die after accidentally overdosing on these drugs. Regular use makes people very weak and damages the lungs and the heart. The drugs can also seriously harm a person's mental health.

Risk of overdose
The most dangerous short-term risk of using cocaine or crack is an overdose. This is when a person takes more of the drug than the body can cope with.

Other short-term risks
Cocaine and crack have many other short-term risks. Users often suffer from headaches, tooth grinding, sweating, difficulty in swallowing, trembling hands, diarrhea, nausea, and vomiting. Use of these drugs can lead to **seizures**. If a person has epilepsy, cocaine and crack can make it much worse.

Cocaine and crack can make people feel overconfident. This can affect their ability to make responsible decisions and could make them do things they would not normally do, such as trusting people they should not trust or getting into fights.

The risks of snorting
Snorting cocaine causes a runny nose, or a nasal drip in which mucus drips down the back of the throat for several hours after the drug has been used. Cocaine also damages the delicate tissues that line the nose, and users may have nosebleeds after taking the drug. If cocaine is used repeatedly, it can cause **ulcers** inside the nose and may even make a hole in the septum of the nose. The septum is the area of skin and cartilage between the nostrils. This damage is irreversible. Snorting cocaine can also cause a loss of sense of smell, **sinusitis**, and chest infections.

Heart and blood vessels

Cocaine and crack put a strain on the heart because they cause an increase in blood pressure. Heavy use of these drugs can lead to chest pains and heart attacks.

People who take cocaine or crack also have an increased risk of having a **stroke**, in which the blood supply is cut off to part of the brain. This may happen because cocaine and crack can cause the brain's blood vessels to close off temporarily. It may also happen because the increase in blood pressure can make blood vessels more likely to tear and cause bleeding into the brain.

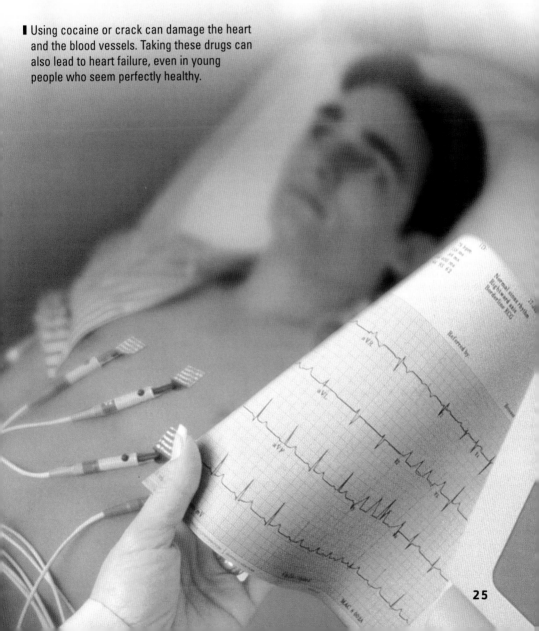

▌ Using cocaine or crack can damage the heart and the blood vessels. Taking these drugs can also lead to heart failure, even in young people who seem perfectly healthy.

Other risks to health

Regular use of cocaine or crack can result in a wide range of other health problems. Some users get stomach cramps, painful ulcers inside their stomachs or long-term problems with indigestion. Cocaine and crack also paralyze the natural cleaning mechanism of the lungs, making infections more likely—including pneumonia and tuberculosis. These drugs can also damage the kidneys and the liver, which are vital organs that remove **toxins** from the body and keep us alive.

Rubbing cocaine into the gums eventually damages these soft tissues and scratches enamel from the surface of the teeth. Smoking crack can cause coughs or sore throats and make asthma worse. Long-term use can lead to a hoarse voice and to chest infections such as bronchitis.

Effects on overall health

People who regularly use cocaine or crack often have generally unhealthy lifestyles. Cocaine and crack users often stay up late at night and may skip meals or eat unhealthy food. When people do not sleep, eat, or rest properly, they quickly become weak and sick. They start to look worn out and their skin may start to look pale and dull. Users also find it hard to fight off infections, so they may suffer from colds, the flu, or sore throats more often than people who do not use drugs.

Yasmine Bleeth's story

Actor Yasmine Bleeth, best known for her appearances on the television programs *Baywatch* and *Nash Bridges,* developed a dependence on cocaine that almost ruined her life. After relationship problems in 1998, she started using drugs frequently, damaging her health, her looks, and many of her friendships. In 2001, Jasmine was arrested after a car accident. She had been using cocaine at the time of the accident. Since the accident, she has gone through a long and difficult period of quitting drug use. During an interview, she discussed her cocaine use:

"It was all I could think about—coming home from work at around eight, locking the door, pulling down the shades, putting on dance music, and doing some lines. . . . My friends said I looked like an alien, that my eyes were bulging out of my face. My looks were the last thing on my mind at the time, but the changes were more than superficial. I just looked . . . dead. Those drugs took all the animation away from my face, all the light from behind my eyes."

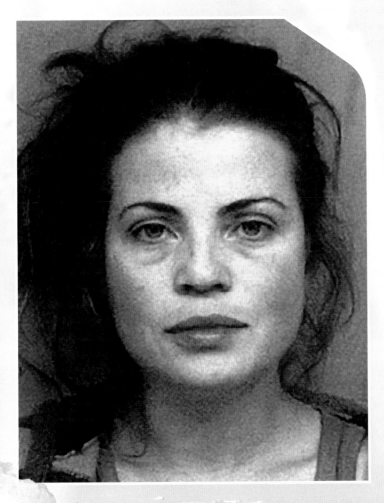

▌The picture on the far left shows actor Yasmine Bleeth in 1996. The picture on the right shows her in 2001 after a period of cocaine dependence.

Risks to mental health

Like any drug that affects a person's brain, cocaine and crack can have very serious short-term and long-term effects on the mind. People who have existing mental health problems, such as depression or anxiety, face an increased risk of those problems getting worse.

Anxiety and panic

While people are under the influence of these drugs, they may feel anxious, tense, and stressed. They may also feel shaky, frightened, "wired," and unable to calm down. These feelings may continue for some time after the drug has been used. Some people have long-term problems, including general feelings of anxiety or sudden strong feelings of panic.

Depression

After the effects of cocaine or crack wear off, the user often feels depressed. Depression is especially common after

someone uses crack. Users may feel "wiped out," tired, or miserable. The longer someone continues to use cocaine or crack, the more likely he or she will suffer from serious depression. Many people feel severely unhappy for very long periods, lose interest in things they normally enjoy, and may start to think that life is not worth living. Worst of all, some users become suicidal.

Other long-term mental health problems

Long-term use of cocaine or crack can result in many kinds of personality, memory, and mood changes. Some users have difficulty remembering things. Others become increasingly arrogant, selfish, stubborn, or irritable.

Many cocaine and crack users lose interest in their friends or become suspicious of the people around them. They may have feelings of **paranoia**, when they believe that someone or something is trying to harm them, control them, or cheat them. They may also start to have several types of irrational beliefs called delusions. Users may become a danger to themselves or others. They may also have **hallucinations**. The paranoia, hallucinations, and delusions sometimes contribute to a user developing a condition known as **cocaine psychosis**.

Alan's story

Alan is a twenty-year-old student. His father is a musician who started using cocaine when he was offered it by his friends.

"Gradually, he began to take more and more cocaine. He stopped working. He started to be violent and abusive to my mom. I lost all respect for him then. I've left home now and I haven't seen my dad for years. We have no relationship. I'd never touch cocaine. It does too much damage."

❚ Cocaine and crack leave many people battling with long-lasting feelings of anxiety or depression.

People die every year after using cocaine and crack, and many others are taken to emergency rooms. Mixing cocaine or crack with alcohol or other drugs also increases the risk of death.

Main causes of death

Cocaine or crack can cause sudden death—there is no way to predict who will die in this way. Most deaths from cocaine or crack use are due to overdoses that lead to heart failure or strokes. Mixing cocaine or crack with other drugs can also be fatal. It is especially dangerous when people mix heroin and cocaine, known as a "speedball," or cocaine or crack with alcohol.

Overdoses

An overdose happens when a person takes more drugs than the body can cope with. This causes a huge rise in blood pressure and body temperature, which leads to fatal heart or lung failure, kidney failure, or a stroke. Signs of an overdose include confusion, dizziness, a dry throat, irregular breathing, hot skin or a flushed face, and seizures.

Question

Why is it so dangerous to mix cocaine and alcohol?

What to do in an emergency

If you think that someone might have overdosed on cocaine or crack, immediately call an ambulance. While you are waiting for the ambulance, get the overdose victim to sit quietly or lie down. Do not give the individual any liquids, food, or drugs. Splash the person with cool water or put a damp towel around him or her if the person is hot. If the person is having a seizure, try to turn him or her onto one side and put a cushion or coat under the head. If the person is not conscious, lie him or her on the left side with the right elbow and right knee bent. This is known as the recovery position.

When the paramedics arrive, give them as much information as you can. Tell them what the person has taken—this could save a life and it will not get you or the overdose victim into trouble.

⚠ Cocaine emergencies

- According to the Drug Abuse Warning Network (DAWN), cocaine-related emergency room visits increased by 47 percent between 1995 and 2002 in the United States. DAWN is a public health organization that tracks the number of drug-related visits to emergency rooms in major cities in the United States.

▌An overdose of cocaine or crack sometimes ends in death. But if paramedics reach the person quickly, they may be able to save a life.

Answer

When the liver tries to break down alcohol and cocaine at the same time, it produces a chemical called cocaethylene. This chemical is poisonous to the heart and it increases the risk of heart attacks and stroke.

Some people take cocaine or crack by injecting them into their bodies with a needle. This method greatly increases the chance of accidentally overdosing. It also causes damage to veins and can lead to the spread of life-threatening diseases.

Why is injecting so risky?

When people inject cocaine or crack into their veins, the drug enters the bloodstream all at once. This means there is an increased risk of overdose, because users may accidentally inject themselves with more than the body can cope with.

Injecting cocaine or crack can also lead to scarring, skin infections, open sores, and **abscesses**. It is also possible to inject poisons, bacteria, and bubbles of air directly into the bloodstream. This can cause serious damage to the veins and block the blood supply to the body's tissues.

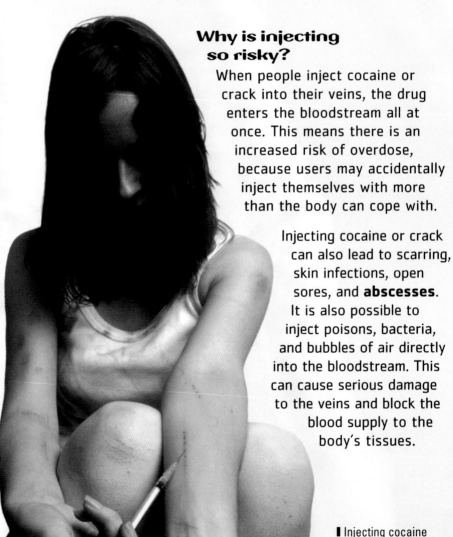

❚ Injecting cocaine or crack can lead to life-threatening infections and accidental overdoses.

In some cases, this can lead to people losing fingers, toes, or legs.

Shared needles

When users share needles, any infection in one person's blood can easily be passed to another person. This means that **HIV** (the virus that causes AIDS) and **hepatitis B** and **C** (which can cause liver disease) can be spread between users.

Needle exchange programs

People who inject drugs often do not have access to clean needles and syringes, which increases the risk of infection. Some health centers now offer clean needles to drug users to prevent the spread of HIV and other infections. People bring their used needles to be safely disposed of and are then given clean needles and health information. Some studies have suggested that needle exchange programs significantly reduce the spread of HIV.

⚠ Reducing the spread of HIV

An evaluation of a needle exchange program in New Haven, Connecticut, showed that the program had reduced the rate of new HIV cases among injecting addicts in the area by about 33 percent.

Viewpoints

In the Netherlands the government provides injecting rooms, where users can inject drugs such as cocaine and crack. Users are given clean needles and advice about safe ways to inject. However, not everyone is in favor of injecting rooms.

- **Injecting rooms reduce the harm caused by injecting drugs**
It is better for drug users to take drugs in a safe environment, away from the general public. The staff are trained to help users if anything goes wrong, and they can give advice about quitting. Injecting rooms do not encourage drug use. The people who use the rooms would be taking drugs anyway.

- **Injecting rooms send out the wrong message**
These drugs are illegal and people should not be allowed to use them anywhere. Providing places for users to take illegal drugs gives out a message that it is OK to use them. Injecting rooms encourage people to take more drugs.

What do you think?

33

Using crack and cocaine can be very harmful to a user's health, but it can also seriously affect many other aspects of his or her life. It causes distress and problems for families, friends, and entire communities.

The effects of dependence

When people become dependent on cocaine or crack, the drugs can quickly start to take over their lives. They may spend so much time thinking about taking drugs that they neglect themselves. They may be unable to manage everyday tasks, such as preparing food. They may also become unreliable at work, which may lead to the loss of their jobs.

Cocaine, crack, and pregnancy

If a woman uses cocaine or crack while she is pregnant, there is an increased risk that she will have a **miscarriage**. People who use drugs while they are pregnant are also more likely to give birth to babies too early. Many babies of cocaine or crack users are seriously underweight when they are born. Sometimes babies show signs that they are dependent on cocaine or crack. They become used to receiving a regular supply of the drug through the mothers' blood.

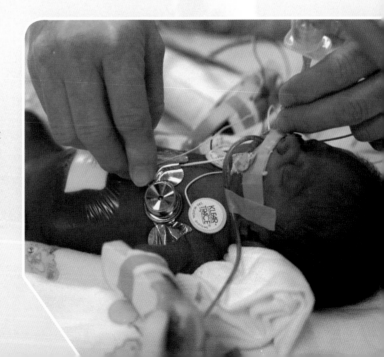

❚ Babies who are born dependent on cocaine or crack need expert medical care and treatment to get them used to not being dependent on the drug.

■ When people regularly use cocaine or crack, they often suffer from mood swings and irritability. This can seriously affect their relationships with friends.

Turning to crime

Taking expensive drugs often causes people to quickly get into unmanageable debt. They may have problems paying rent, mortgages, or other bills. They may even lose their homes or be taken to court. Some people resort to selling their possessions to get money to help fund their habits. Others become drug dealers or turn to other forms of crime, including mugging, burglary, and stealing from friends, relatives, or employers. Some people get involved in prostitution to earn money for drugs.

Friends and family

The people close to a drug user suffer too. Cocaine or crack users often spend more and more time with their drug-using friends and less time with their families and former friends. Mood swings and disturbed sleeping and eating patterns can make a drug user very hard to get along with. Some people who use cocaine and crack become angry and violent and lash out at loved ones or attack them when they are feeling paranoid.

The effects upon a community

A whole community can be affected when cocaine or crack are being abused—even when they are used by a small number of individuals. Non-drug users may feel afraid of drug dealers in the area and of violence between rival drug gangs. This can affect innocent people. Drug users may steal or use violence to get money to buy cocaine and crack, and many local people become the victims of crimes. Elderly people often live in fear of violent crime related to drugs.

The cost of drug crime

Drug-related crimes take up a large amount of police time. Police officers have to arrest people who sell, buy, or use cocaine or crack. They also have to investigate drug-related crimes, such as car thefts, muggings, and burglaries, and try to catch the people who have committed these offenses. Police officers and specially trained drug squads work hard to trace the movements of drugs and the criminal gangs that control the drug trade. Governments all around the world spend large amounts of money to try to prosecute the traffickers, dealers, and users of illegal drugs, and on keeping them in prison if they are found guilty. In the United States, 70 percent of people held in prison are there because of drug-related crimes.

▌These Colombian officers are searching for drug smugglers. Police operations such as this often take months to set up and involve many officers.

Medical care

The criminal justice system is not the only system strained by drug use. Every year, thousands of people need emergency medical care because of the use of cocaine or crack. Some users also need long-term medical treatment for problems they suffer after using cocaine or crack. These problems take up the time and resources of doctors, nurses, clinics, and hospitals and take medical professionals away from their work with other patients.

Everyone pays

Customs officers, the police, and medical professionals all must work hard to deal with the problems associated with cocaine and crack abuse. All the extra work involved in tackling illegal drug use has to be paid for by individuals, often through tax increases.

▌Emergencies and long-term medical problems caused by cocaine and crack abuse put medical staff under extra pressure.

"I see people in court all the time who have been stealing to get money for drugs. The penalties can be serious—and just as seriously they end up with a criminal record, which could stop them from doing the things they want to do in life."

Karen, a judge

Cocaine and crack are illegal drugs—it is illegal to make them, sell them, give them away, or **possess** them. Governments around the world impose strict penalties for these crimes, and a conviction for a drug offense can seriously affect a person's future. Not knowing the laws is not an excuse that can be given in court.

Cocaine laws in the United States

Cocaine was one of the first drugs to be made illegal in the United States. The first federal, or national, laws concerning cocaine were passed in 1914. These laws gave criminal uses of cocaine the same penalties as were given to illegal uses of opium, morphine, and heroin. The United States Congress classified cocaine as a Schedule II drug in 1970. Schedule II drugs are classified as such because they have a high potential for abuse. There is also a great chance that people who use Schedule II drugs will develop a strong physical or psychological dependence on the drugs.

❚ Officers with specially trained dogs are sometimes allowed into schools to combat drug use. Students may have their clothes, bags, or lockers searched.

Question

Can someone get in trouble if they hold or hide drugs for a friend?

Crack cocaine laws

In general, people caught using or selling crack are subject to harsher penalties than those caught using or selling cocaine. According to federal law, someone caught with only 0.2 ounces (5 grams) of crack cocaine is subject to an automatic sentence of five years in prison. Possession of a similar amount of cocaine can result in a prison sentence of

▌ Gilberto Rodriguez Orejuela was the head of one of the largest drug-trafficking cartels in the world. He is shown in this photograph at the airport in Bogota, Colombia, after the president of Colombia agreed to turn him over to the U.S. Drug Enforcement Agency in 2004.

up to a year, but is more likely to lead to a fine. Cocaine and crack are also covered by laws that are passed by individual states, so certain offenses may be a crime in some states but not in others. The punishments in each state vary.

Trafficking

Transporting or smuggling illegal drugs in large amounts between different states or countries is known as trafficking. Carrying drugs across international borders and state lines can lead to severe punishments, including long prison sentences. Sometimes people are tricked into transporting drugs across borders by others, but they are still committing a crime. The United States and Mexico border is the main entry point for the cocaine that is illegally brought into the United States. About 65 percent of the cocaine entering the United States is smuggled into the country at this border.

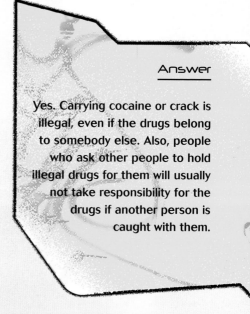

Answer

Yes. Carrying cocaine or crack is illegal, even if the drugs belong to somebody else. Also, people who ask other people to hold illegal drugs for them will usually not take responsibility for the drugs if another person is caught with them.

▌Police officers can stop and search anyone they have reason to think might be carrying drugs. An arrest for possessing a large amount of cocaine can lead to someone being prosecuted for intention to sell the cocaine.

The powers of the police and courts

If police officers or other authorities catch someone who is carrying cocaine or crack, they can seize the drugs, or take them away, according to the law. They can also seize equipment that might be used to measure or use the drugs. The person may then be arrested and taken to court. A court usually decides what penalty the person should be given.

"It was a once-in-a-lifetime opportunity when I was offered the chance to travel to Japan with some friends in 2003. But I could not get permission to travel to Japan from the Japanese authorities because I have a previous conviction for cocaine possession. Getting caught with a tiny amount of cocaine, something that happened six years ago, meant I had to stay home while all my friends went to Japan and had a great time."

Zac, age 24

Young offenders are sometimes very lucky and may only be given a warning or put into a treatment program. If someone is older, however, or has committed a more serious crime, the punishment may be tougher. They may be sent to prison, or made to pay a severe fine. Drug dealers and traffickers can also have their homes and possessions taken away by the courts.

Drug seizures in the United States

There is an amazing amount of cocaine and crack seized by government officials every year in the United States. Federal authorities are constantly trying to stop the distribution of these drugs. United States federal law enforcement authorities seized 233,436 pounds (105,885 kilograms) of cocaine in 2001 and 134,204 pounds (60,874 kilograms) from January to September 2002. The drug seizures and the resulting automatic prison sentences for crack possession and dealing have caused crack dealers and distributors to not move or smuggle crack over long distances or in large amounts. Crack is usually converted from powder cocaine closer to the areas where it is sold.

What a drug conviction can mean

If someone is arrested for a drug crime, they can end up with a criminal record. A criminal record could prevent someone from getting a dream job. Some countries refuse to allow anyone with a drug conviction to travel to the country. As a result, drug convictions can also stop people from traveling freely, even for a business trip or a vacation.

▌Being caught with a relatively small amount of cocaine or crack can lead to time in prison or fines.

Preventing Cocaine and Crack Abuse

Governments have passed strict laws that send out a clear message that cocaine and crack are illegal, but what else can be done to prevent cocaine and crack abuse? Communities, schools, and governments all have to work together to tackle this difficult problem.

Helping local communities

Many programs exist to help reduce the amount of cocaine and crack use in communities. Some health centers run drug outreach programs, in which trained staff members go to areas where there have been drug problems in the past. They educate people about the risks of drugs and give out information to people who want to quit using drugs. Some community organizations do not directly target drug use, but they can still help to reduce drug use.

▌Many schools run drug education programs, in which students are encouraged to talk about drugs and develop strategies for coping with peer pressure and peer influence.

For example, a plan that improves local employment prospects may help people stop using or selling drugs, perhaps by reducing poverty, raising self-esteem, or giving people a sense of purpose.

Schools and education

Many schools have drug education lessons about cocaine, crack, and other drugs. Some schools arrange visits from officers from drug education programs. Providing honest information and friendly advice seems to be an effective way to educate young people about drugs. Some schools operate programs where older students are trained to educate, or mentor, younger students. Projects and programs that help young people increase their self-esteem and gain more confidence will help them make healthier choices.

"Drug education is important—but you can't preach at kids and tell them what to do. You have to give them the information and then help them develop the confidence to make their own decisions. The rest is up to them."

Sarah, drug education worker

Zero tolerance

Many schools operate "zero tolerance" policies toward students who use drugs. This means that students caught using drugs will be automatically punished. They may be expelled, or excluded from certain activities. Some people believe that this approach helps to reduce the number of young people who use drugs. However, some experts suggest that the zero tolerance approach may make drug-taking worse among certain groups of students.

A tough approach?

Some governments hope that harsh sentences will put people off using drugs. In the United States, judges sometimes give drug users a choice—get treatment for your drug problem or go to prison. Ex-users may then have to take regular drug tests to prove that they have completely given up cocaine or crack.

Some countries have taken a different approach. They have reduced the punishment for users and have increased the amount of support available for people who are dependent on these drugs instead.

▋American troops have helped the Colombian government spray large areas where coca crops are being grown.

❗ Reduced supply

The amount of coca grown in the Andean region has decreased steadily over the last few years, falling by 30 percent between 1999 and 2003. This may be partly because of the destruction of coca crops and partly because alternative development programs have enabled farmers to grow legal crops instead.

Cutting down the supply

To help cut down the supply of illegal drugs, many countries work together to prevent trafficking and large-scale drug dealing. International police forces and anti-drug agencies share information with one another to do this. In recent years, many countries have introduced tight border controls in an attempt to prevent drug smuggling. However, customs and police officers in the United States say that only about 10 percent of illegal drugs entering the country are detected.

The war on drugs

President Ronald Reagan first declared a "war on drugs" in 1982. This government campaign aims to reduce drug abuse. Tough methods are used to cut down the supply of drugs. Millions of dollars are spent to destroy coca crops in South America and illegal drug factories. The United States has also provided financial and military support to South American governments to fight drugs. Many governments now cooperate on this issue.

Alternative development programs

The "alternative development" approach aims to reduce the supply of cocaine by encouraging farmers in South America to grow legal crops instead of coca. Development programs provide money to plant legal crops such as coffee or pineapples. Farmers are given help to sell their goods for the best price possible.

▌Farmers need to make a living, and some of them have agreed to join programs that enable them to get a fair income from growing legal crops such as coffee.

Viewpoints

The United States has helped the Colombian government to spray coca fields with chemicals in order to destroy them. Not everyone thinks this is a good way to prevent drug abuse.

- **Spraying crops helps to reduce the supply of cocaine**
  Killing coca plants prevents the crop from being turned into cocaine. Wiping out all the coca farms in one area sends a strong message to farmers and drug cartels. Farmers are less likely to grow coca crops if they think they will be destroyed.

- **Spraying crops is not the best solution**
  Spraying coca crops cannot cut off the supply of cocaine because it would be impossible to spray all the coca plants in South America. Crop spraying has harmed the health of people and animals. Coca spraying has also damaged the environment of South America. Poor farmers should be helped, so that they can earn enough money from growing legal crops.

What do you think? 45

People can develop a strong dependence on cocaine and crack, so it can be hard to quit using these drugs. Fortunately, there is a lot of help and support available for people who want to break free from cocaine and crack.

The first steps

Many drug **counselors** say that the first important step toward quitting is for the person to admit that they have a problem with drugs. The next step for many people is to talk to a family doctor, who can refer them to a drug service or hospital unit that specializes in drug dependence.

Treatment for dependence

If cocaine or crack have become central to a person's life, it can be hard for them to cope without these drugs. They need to find ways to deal with their cravings and resist the temptation to take the drug again.

Some people go through the process of giving up by staying at a hospital or drug treatment center for four to six weeks. These programs may include individual and group therapy sessions, skills training, and confidence building.

▮ Some people find group therapy helps them quit using cocaine or crack and stay away from the drugs forever. These groups are often run by people who are ex-users.

Many people find that counseling helps. During counseling, people can talk through their problems privately and work out ways to cope without drugs. Others are greatly helped by **behavioral therapy**. This is a type of counseling that involves trying to find ways to change people's behavior so that they can find healthier ways to deal with their problems.

Rehabilitation

Rehabilitation is the process of getting someone's life back together after a period of dependence. This will often include solving money, housing, or employment problems. Family relationships may need to be mended. Ex-users will need to make new friends and to avoid people who are still using cocaine and crack.

I Cocaine and crack are not part of a healthy lifestyle. Many people who have quit taking drugs take pride in getting physically fit.

Simone's story

Simone started smoking crack when she was eighteen. It eventually took over her life and she dropped out of school.

"Finally, I called a drug program and asked for help. I moved into a live-in treatment program. Now I'm growing up, I'm learning to accept limits, taking care of my friends, and trying to fix things that are not right. Most of all I've learned to express myself."

Your decisions about drugs can affect the rest of your life. At some time in the future, you may find yourself under pressure to take cocaine or crack. You may not want to try them, but explaining that to a persuasive friend or dealer may be hard. It's a good idea to plan ahead for how you will cope with that situation.

Serious consequences

As we have seen, cocaine and crack can damage a person's life in many ways. These drugs can seriously harm a person's health, and when someone becomes dependent on them, it can also damage a person's relationships and prospects in life. A criminal record for a drug offense may ruin a person's chances of getting a good job, going to college, or traveling to foreign countries.

Making healthy choices

It is normal to want to fit in with friends, but if your friends are using drugs, you don't have to copy their behavior. True friends will respect you for making your own decisions. Remember that the vast majority of young people never take illegal drugs, not even once. It is up to you to make healthy choices in your life. For example, if you think you lack confidence, you could join a drama club or try learning a martial art. If you feel bored, you could take up a new sport, start a band, or raise money for a cause you feel strongly about.

Under pressure?

If someone tries to force you to take drugs, or drug dealers start hanging around your school, it can feel scary. You don't have to deal with situations like this on your own, especially if you are feeling threatened. Tell an adult—parents, teachers, or the police can be helpful. Hotlines will also give you advice.

❚ The majority of young people choose to have fun in ways that don't involve drugs.

Thinking ahead

One day you might be offered cocaine or crack by a friend or a dealer. It helps to be prepared and think about what you'll say in advance. If someone tries to pressurize you, remember:

- saying "No thanks" or "I'm not interested" is usually enough.
- if someone keeps bothering you, say "No thanks" again or explain why you don't want to take drugs.
- if they won't stop, walk away from the person.
- whatever people say, it's OK to say no to drugs.
- no one can tell you what to do—it's your life, you are in control, and you make your own decisions.

Are there things that worry you about cocaine or crack? Maybe you are worried about somebody else who might be using these drugs? Fortunately, there are many people and places you can contact.

Finding out more

You might like to read some leaflets or booklets about cocaine, crack, or other drugs. These may be available at your school or at a nearby health center or library. You can also find them at youth clubs and some health clubs. Many schools now have special lessons where teachers or trained drug educators have discussions about drug issues. Students are encouraged to join, and more information is available for those who want it. You can also borrow books from your school library.

Talking it through

If you're still worried about anything to do with drugs, remember that you won't get into trouble for asking questions. It might seem difficult to start talking sometimes, but you'll feel much better if you talk about your concerns. Many schools have a nurse or **counselor** who is aware of drug issues. There are also many organizations that offer help and advice about drug-related problems. You will find out more information about these organizations on pages 54–55 of this book.

Some organizations run telephone hotlines, staffed by specially trained, understanding advisers. Some hotlines are open 24 hours a day. This means you can call them any time—even if you have a problem in the middle of the night. Hotline services are completely confidential, so what you say will not be talked about with anyone you know.

Worried about someone else's drug use?

If you are concerned that someone close to you is using cocaine or crack, it is a good idea to talk to him or her openly and honestly and encourage the person to seek help and support. Don't feel you have to bottle your feelings up and try to cope on your own. A number of organizations have been set up to give support and advice to people who have a friend, partner, or relative with a drug problem.

▍Telephone hotline operators are specially trained to listen carefully to your concerns and questions. Their advice is both professional and confidential.

Glossary

abscess inflamed pus-filled swelling

abuse use of drugs for nonmedical reasons, usually in an excessive manner

addiction when a person is unable to manage without a drug, and finds it extremely hard to stop using a drug. A person who is addicted to a drug is known as an addict.

anesthetic drug that causes loss of sensation of pain

behavioral therapy type of counseling that involves helping someone change a behavior to find healthy ways to cope with problems

blood pressure pressure of the blood as it circulates around the body

cartel group of people trading a particular product who try to control world prices for the product

cocaine hydrochloride chemical name for cocaine powder

cocaine psychosis serious mental disorder in which a person loses touch with reality and experiences strong feelings of paranoia or hallucinations as a result of cocaine abuse

counseling advice and guidance given to people to help resolve their problems. A person trained to give advice and guidance to people to help resolve their problems is called a counselor.

courier someone who carries drugs across a border for somebody else

craving strong or uncontrollable need or longing for something

dealer person who buys and sells illegal drugs

dependence when a person is unable to cope without a drug

drug baron someone who controls the growing, smuggling, and selling of drugs

freebase another name for crack cocaine

hallucination experience of seeing or hearing something that is not really present and only exists in the mind

hepatitis B and **C** diseases caused by a virus that can seriously damage the liver

high feeling of happiness, relaxation, or calmness

hit dose of a drug that is being abused

HIV virus that can lead to AIDS

lethargy lack of energy and enthusiasm

media television, film, magazines, newspapers, and any other forms of mass communication

miscarriage loss of a baby because it has died inside the womb, usually early in pregnancy

mule someone who carries illegal drugs over a border. Mules sometimes swallow small packages containing drugs.

nausea feeling of wanting to vomit

overdose excessive dose of a drug, which the body cannot cope with

paranoia mental condition involving feelings of suspicion and distrust— a sense that everyone is out to get you or criticize your behavior or actions

possession owning or having an illegal drug (either carrying it or having it hidden somewhere)

psychological dependence when a person feels a need for drugs to get through everyday life and cannot cope without them

rave all-night party, often staged illegally, where dance music is played

rehabilitation process of returning to ordinary healthy life after a period of addiction

seizure sudden attack that causes the body to go into spasm (also known as a convulsion)

sinusitis inflammation of the sinuses

snort take a drug by sniffing it up the nose

stimulant drug that speeds up the activity of the brain, making people feel alert and full of energy

stroke sudden change in the blood supply to part of the brain, which can cause loss of physical functions such as movement or speech

tolerance need for larger and larger doses of a drug to get the same effect

toxin poison

trafficking smuggling or transporting drugs, usually in large amounts and across the borders of different countries

ulcer open sore that heals very slowly

Contacts and Further Reading

There are a number of organizations that provide information and advice about cocaine and crack. Some provide information packs and leaflets, while others offer help and support over the phone.

Contacts

American Council for Drug Education (ACDE)
164 W. 74th Street
New York, NY 10023
Tel.: (800) 488-3784

ACDE is a substance abuse prevention and education agency that develops programs and materials for teens. It also provides information to parents and teachers.

Cocaine Anonymous
3740 Overland Ave., Suite C
Los Angeles, CA 90034
Tel.: (310) 559-5833

Cocaine Anonymous is a organization made up of people who have quit using cocaine, using a twelve-step program similar to the one used by Alcoholics Anonymous. They have a hotline for users and their friends and relatives, plus events and meetings around the United States.

DARE America
9800 La Cienega Blvd., Suite 401
Inglewood, CA 90301
Tel.: (800) 223-DARE

Drug Abuse Resistance Education (DARE) runs educational programs to help young people resist the pressures that might cause them to experiment with drugs, including crack and cocaine.

Drug Free AZ
301 W. Jefferson, Suite 8
Phoenix, AZ 85003
Tel.: (602) 506-7630

Drug Free AZ started in 2002 with the main goal of keeping young people from starting to use drugs and convincing occasional users to stop.

National Clearinghouse for Alcohol and Drug Information
11420 Rockville Pike
Rockville, MD 20852
Tel.: (800)-729-6686 (24 hours a day)

This is a great resource for information about substance abuse prevention and addiction treatment.

National Council on Alcoholism and Drug Dependence, Inc. (NCADD)
20 Exchange Place, Suite 2902
New York, NY 10005
Tel.: (212) 269-7797
Tel.: (800) 622-2255

NCADD offers educational materials and information on drugs. It has a national hotline and also provides phone numbers of local NCADD affiliates who can provide information on local treatment resources.

National Youth Crisis Hotline
Tel.: (800) 448-4663

This hotline offers confidential help and guidance for young people on a range of worries and problems, including problems caused by cocaine.

Partnership for a Drug-Free America
405 Lexington Ave., Suite 1601
New York, NY 10174
Tel.: (212) 922-1560

The Partnership for a Drug-Free America is a nonprofit organization of communication, health, medical, and educational professionals working to reduce illicit drug use and help people live healthy, drug-free lives.

Further reading

Barter, James. *Cocaine and Crack*. San Diego: Lucent Books, 2001.

Bayer, Linda N. *Crack & Cocaine*. Broomall, Pa.: Chelsea House Publishers, 2000.

Connolly, Sean. *Just the Facts: Cocaine*. Chicago: Heinemann Library, 2000.

Constant, Clare. *Teen Issues: Drugs*. Chicago: Raintree, 2005.

Lennard-Brown, Sarah. *Health Issues: Cocaine*. Chicago: Raintree, 2005.

McFarland, Rhodda. *Cocaine*. New York: Rosen Publishing, 2000.

Palenque, Stephanie Maher. *Crack & Cocaine = Busted!* Berkeley Heights, N.J.: Enslow Publishers, 2005.

Westcott, Patsy. *Why Do People Take Drugs?* Chicago: Raintree, 2001.

Index